AF228624

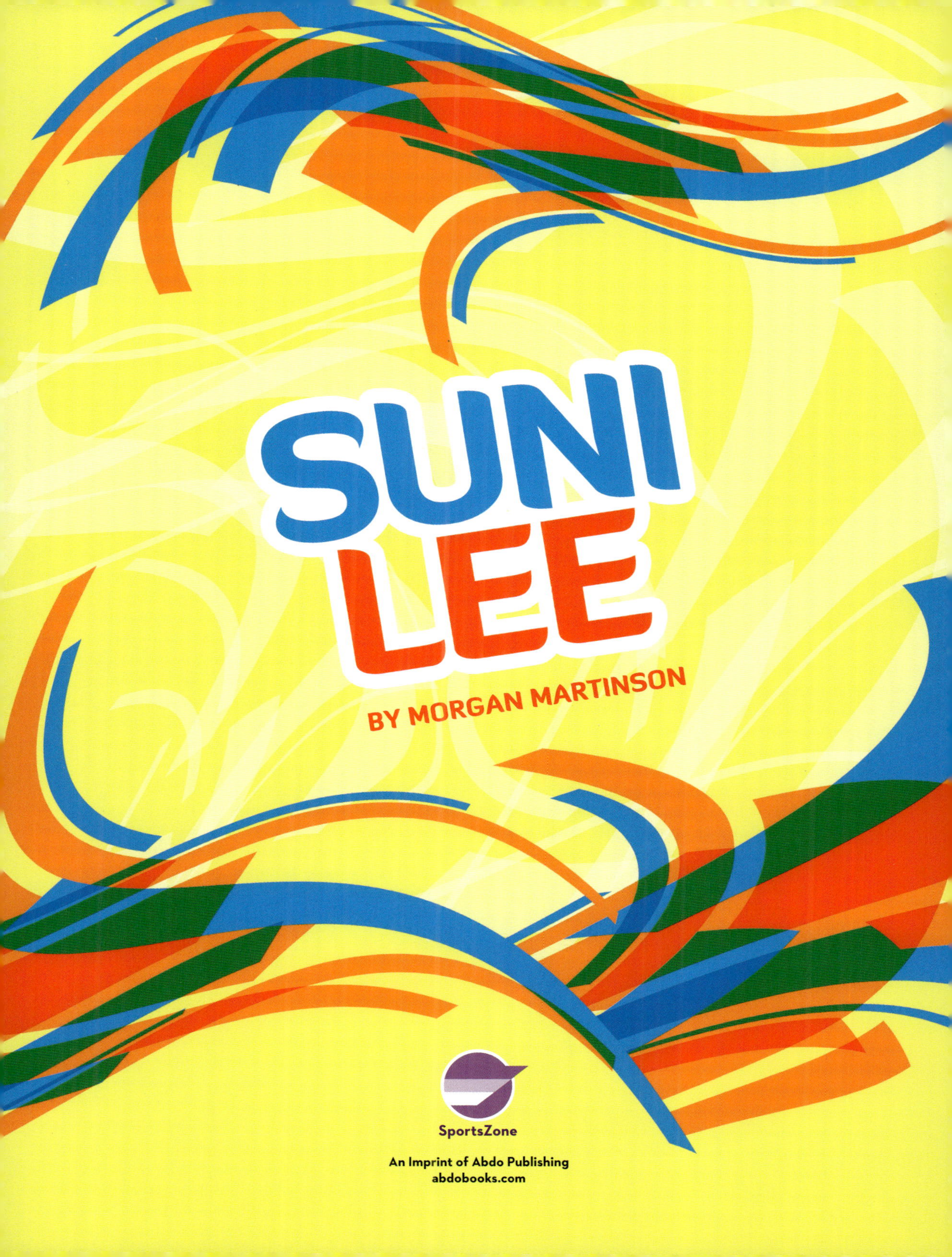

SUNI LEE

BY MORGAN MARTINSON

SportsZone

An Imprint of Abdo Publishing
abdobooks.com

abdobooks.com

Published by Abdo Publishing, a division of ABDO, PO Box 398166, Minneapolis, Minnesota 55439. Copyright © 2022 by Abdo Consulting Group, Inc. International copyrights reserved in all countries. No part of this book may be reproduced in any form without written permission from the publisher. SportsZone™ is a trademark and logo of Abdo Publishing.

Printed in the United States of America, North Mankato, Minnesota.
102021
012022

THIS BOOK CONTAINS RECYCLED MATERIALS

Cover Photo: Alexey Filippov/Sputnik/AP Images
Interior Photos: Morry Gash/AP Images, 4-5; Frank Hoermann/Sven Simon/picture-alliance/dpa/AP Images, 6-7, 8-9, 19; Escoda/AP Images, 10; Evan Frost/Minnesota Public Radio/AP Images, 11, 12-13; Melissa J. Perenson/Cal Sport Media/AP Images, 14; Charlie Riedel/AP Images, 15, 18; Christine T. Nguyen/Minnesota Public Radio/AP Images, 16-17, 20; Yomiuri Shimbun/AP Images, 21; Jeff Roberson/AP Images, 22-23; Pete Dovgan/Speed Media/Icon Sportswire/AP Images, 24-25; Elizabeth Flores/Star Tribune/AP Images, 26; Gregory Bull/AP Images, 27; Jerry Holt/Star Tribune/AP Images, 28, 29

Editor: Arnold Ringstad
Series Designer: Jake Nordby

Library of Congress Control Number: 2021945011

Publisher's Cataloging-in-Publication Data

Names: Martinson, Morgan, author.
Title: Suni Lee / by Morgan Martinson
Description: Minneapolis, Minnesota : Abdo Publishing, 2022 | Series: Olympic stars set 3 | Includes online resources and index.
Identifiers: ISBN 9781532197406 (lib. bdg.) | ISBN 9781644947579 (pbk.) | ISBN 9781098219635 (ebook)
Subjects: LCSH: Lee, Sunisa, 2003---Juvenile literature. | Gymnastics--Juvenile literature. | Women gymnasts--Juvenile literature. | Women Olympic athletes--Juvenile literature. | Hmong American women--Juvenile literature. | Asian American athletes--Juvenile literature.
Classification: DDC 796.44092--dc23

CONTENTS

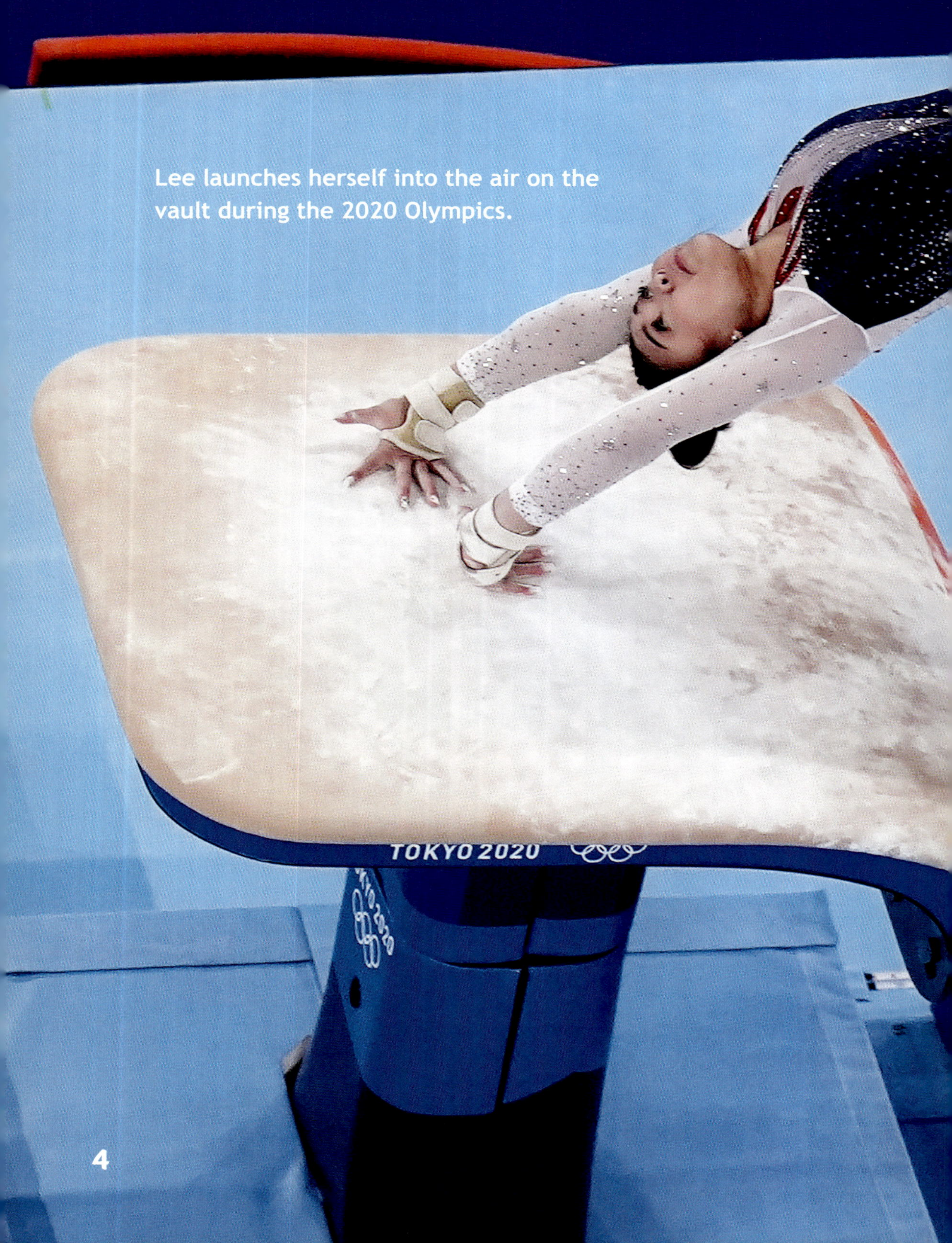

Lee launches herself into the air on the vault during the 2020 Olympics.

ALL-AROUND CHAMP

Suni Lee took a deep breath, then charged ahead at full speed. Just before reaching the vault, she turned into a roundoff. The 18-year-old then performed a back handspring and bounced backward off the springboard. Pushing off the vault and into the air, Lee spun around twice while flipping backward. Landing with a stick, Lee smiled. It was a strong start to the women's all-around competition at the 2020 Olympic Games in Tokyo, Japan.

The competition for gold was fierce. Lee's US teammate Simone Biles came to Tokyo as the favorite. But Biles had withdrawn. Many other gymnasts now believed they could win.

Lee knew her best opportunity to rack up points was on the uneven bars. Few in the world could match her impressive routine. It combined high-flying release moves with tricky combinations as she swung from bar to bar. On this night, Lee performed all her hardest skills. And she nailed the routine. With a score of 15.300, she was less than a point out of first place.

The uneven bars event is Lee's specialty.

FAST FACT
Lee became the fifth US woman in a row to win the Olympic all-around gold medal.

8

On the balance beam, Lee crouched on one foot and spun. The move is called a wolf turn. Spinning on the 4-inch (10-cm) beam is harder than it looks. Lee almost fell off. The routine wasn't as sharp as she'd hoped. Lee took the lead, but just barely.

The pressure was on for floor exercise. Once again, Lee delivered. Then she had to wait for the others to perform. When the final gymnast was done, Lee still had the lead. She was the all-around gold medalist!

Lee wowed the floor exercise judges during the all-around final.

FAST FACT
The Twin Cities of St. Paul
and Minneapolis have the
largest Hmong population
of any area in the United
States. Around 80,000
Hmong live there.

A MINNESOTA KID

During the Vietnam War (1954-1975), the United States needed help. It recruited Hmong people from neighboring Laos to join forces with US troops. After the war, the Hmong were no longer welcome in their homeland. They had become refugees. Many Hmong eventually came to the United States. One of them was Yeev Thoj, who moved to Minnesota in 1987. On March 9, 2003, she gave birth to a daughter named Sunisa. The young girl became known as Suni for short. Yeev's partner, John Lee, helped raise Suni. He had arrived from Laos in 1979.

Suni does homework on the couch with her dad and siblings in 2017.

Minnesota's Hmong community is tight-knit. Extended families are often large. People help each other out. But not everyone understood when John signed Suni up for a gymnastics class. Some in the community thought sports were not something to give too much time to. Suni was six years old. Like many kids her age, she liked to tumble and flip around the house.

Suni practices at a gymnastics center in Minnesota in May 2017.

Suni performs on the balance beam at the 2017 US Classic in Illinois.

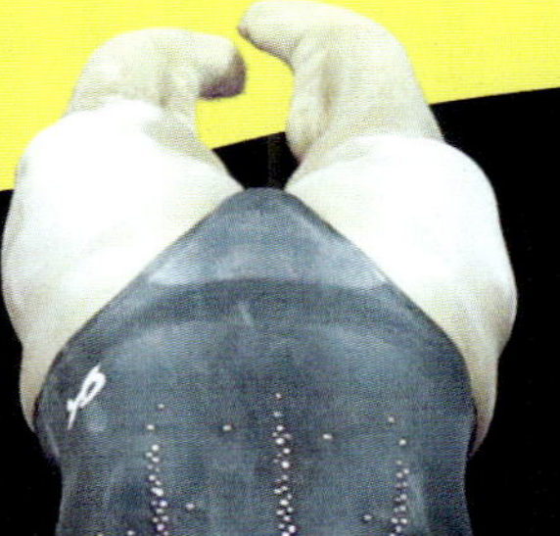

Growing up, Suni's ankles were often injured. That made practicing some gymnastics events difficult. The one event she could always practice, though, was the uneven bars. Suni practiced her bars for hours and hours. Over time she became very skilled. In time, she learned to do one of the most difficult bar routines in the world. Suni was not just a bars specialist, though. She was on her way to becoming an elite all-arounder.

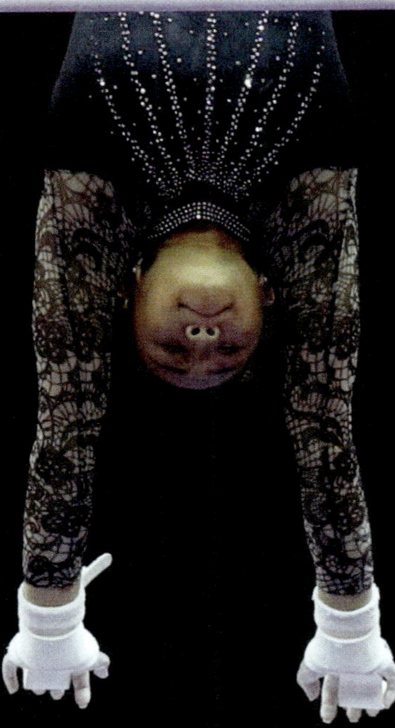

Years of practice sharpened Suni's skills on the uneven bars.

FAST FACT
Lee's dad is her biggest fan. He gives her a pep talk before each competition.

RISING STAR

The summer of 2019 was an important time for Lee. Her first national championships at the senior level were in August. But one day before she left, her dad was injured. John Lee was helping a neighbor trim a tree. The ladder he was using fell over. John became partially paralyzed. Lee begged her parents to let her stay home. But John encouraged her to go compete.

Another US gymnast, Simone Biles, was the best in the world. Everyone expected her to win—and she did. Not far behind in second, however, was Lee. And nobody scored higher than Lee on the uneven bars. After that, Lee was selected to compete in the 2019 World Championships in Germany. She excelled there too. Her scores helped Team USA win the gold medal. Lee also won a silver medal on floor exercise and a bronze medal on the uneven bars. One year out from the 2020 Olympics, she appeared to be a strong favorite to make the US team.

Simone Biles won first place at the 2019 US Championships, but Lee finished a strong second.

Lee swings on the uneven bars during the team final at the 2019 World Championships.

Lee practices at her gym in Little Canada, Minnesota, just a few weeks before widespread closures due to COVID-19 began.

In early 2020, the disease COVID-19 spread around the world. In March many places in the United States closed in response to the pandemic, including Lee's gym and her school. The Olympics were also postponed one year. They would be held in 2021 instead. Lee tried to stay motivated, but it was hard. Two close relatives died from the disease. When she finally got back into the gym, she injured her foot. At times, she wasn't sure she wanted to continue.

COVID-19 led to changes for gymnastics. Everyone had to wear masks, and equipment had to be frequently disinfected.

FAST FACT
Lee became the first
Hmong American to make
a US Olympic team in
any sport.

OLYMPIAN

Lee's foot still hurt when 2021 arrived. Early in the year, she could compete only on the balance beam and uneven bars. By the Olympic trials in June, though, she was at her best. After finishing as the runner-up to Simone Biles there, she was an easy choice for Team USA.

Lee competes on the balance beam at the US Olympic trials in St. Louis, Missouri.

FAST FACT
Fans were not allowed at
the Tokyo Olympics due to
the COVID-19 pandemic.
Instead, more than 200
of Lee's family members
and friends cheered her
on from watch parties in
Minnesota.

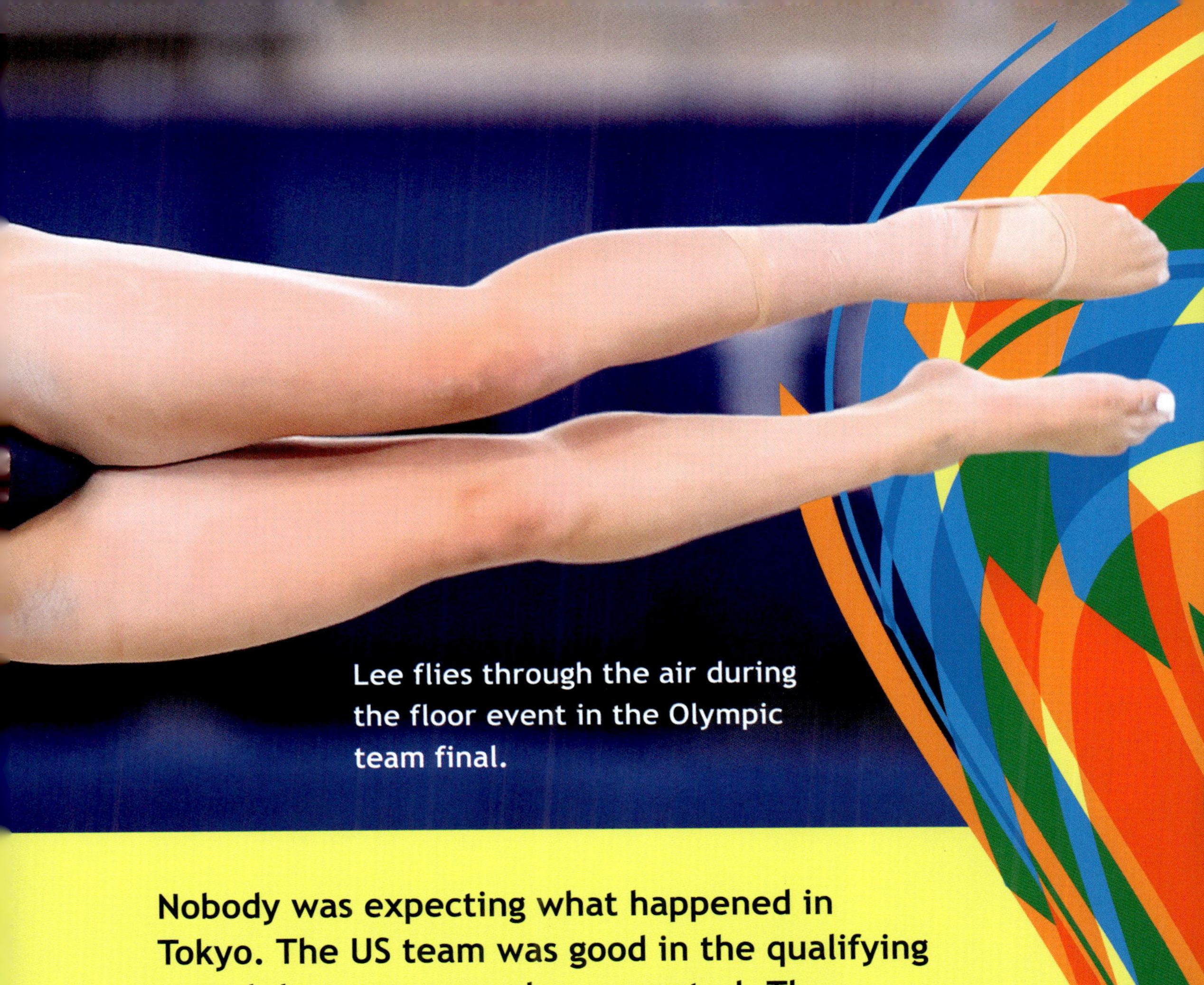

Lee flies through the air during the floor event in the Olympic team final.

Nobody was expecting what happened in Tokyo. The US team was good in the qualifying round, but not as good as expected. Then Biles had to pull out of the team competition. Lee's high-scoring uneven bars routine helped reassure her team. Her sturdy movements on the beam led to another good score. Lee then filled Biles's spot on floor too. Despite not warming up, Lee delivered again. With three strong performances, she helped Team USA win the silver medal.

Two days later, Lee won the all-around gold medal. Winning that medal, one of the most prestigious of the Games, was exciting. People around the world congratulated Lee. Members of the media asked for interviews. She also wanted to celebrate with her teammates. However, all of this made it hard for Lee to prepare for her next event final.

Supporters back home, including Lee's mother, *bottom left*, and father, *right*, celebrated when she won gold.

FAST FACT

After Lee won the all-around gold medal on a Thursday, the governor of Minnesota declared the following Friday to be "Sunisa Lee Day."

Lee posed for photos with her gold medal after her impressive victory.

A parade was held in Lee's honor when she arrived home in Minnesota.

Coming into the Olympics, Lee thought her best chance to win gold was on the uneven bars. But competing three days after the all-around, she struggled to connect her skills as planned. However, her challenging routine still won her a bronze medal. Two days later she finished fifth on the balance beam too.

Lee's Olympic success was historic. People across the United States were proud, especially other Hmong. Lee hoped she inspired her community to follow her example and dream big.

Some fans at Lee's parade wore traditional Hmong clothing.

TIMELINE

1987

Lee's mom, Yeev Thoj, moves to the United States from Laos.

2003

Sunisa Lee is born on March 9 in St. Paul, Minnesota.

2019

In her first senior national championships in August, Lee wins the uneven bars and finishes second to Simone Biles in the all-around.

2019

At the World Championships in October, Lee wins a gold medal with the team as well as a silver medal on floor exercise and a bronze medal on the uneven bars.

2020

The COVID-19 pandemic shuts down much of the United States, including Lee's gym and school.

2020

Organizers announce on March 24 that the upcoming Tokyo Olympics will be postponed to 2021.

2021

In her first all-around competition in more than a year, Lee finishes as runner-up at the national championships. Three weeks later she is runner-up again at the Olympic trials.

2021

After teammate Simone Biles withdraws, Lee steps up in the Olympic team competition and helps the United States win a silver medal on July 27.

2021

On July 29, Lee wins the prestigious Olympic all-around gold medal. Three days later she wins a bronze medal on the uneven bars, her favorite event.

GLOSSARY

all-around
A gymnastics competition in which women compete in all four events.

pandemic
The spread of a disease across a wide area.

paralyzed
Lost the ability to move part of one's body.

prestigious
Having respect and admiration.

recruited
Encouraged to join a cause.

refugee
A person who is forced to leave his or her homeland due to unfair treatment or violence.

release moves
Gymnastics skills in which the athlete lets go of the bar, performs a movement, and then grabs back onto the bar.

roundoff
A gymnastics move in which someone goes from their hands to their feet and back to their hands while making a half twist.

routine
A set performance by a gymnast in one event.

stick
When a gymnast lands on the mat following a routine without moving her feet.

INDEX

Online Resources

To learn more about Suni Lee, please visit **abdobooklinks.com** or scan this QR code. These links are routinely monitored and updated to provide the most current information available.

About the Author

Morgan Martinson is a writer from Seattle, Washington, who has been writing about the Olympics and other sports for many years.